I0782979

Mastering the Art of Persuasion and Argument:

Unlocking the Power of Influence and Reasoning for Personal and Professional Triumph

By

Brandon Y. Doherty

**Copyright © by Brandon Y. Doherty 2024.
All rights reserved.**

Before this document is duplicated or reproduced in any manner, the publisher's consent must be gained. Therefore, the contents within can neither be stored electronically, transferred, nor kept in a database. Neither in Part nor full can the document be copied, scanned, faxed, or retained without approval from the publisher or creator.

Mastering the Art of Persuasion and Argument

TABLE OF CONTENTS

Introduction

Persuasion and argumentation are two of the threads that weave together a captivating narrative that molds our views, decisions, and relationships. This narrative is woven into the intricate tapestry that is human communication. The book "Understanding the Foundations of Persuasion and Argumentation" takes the reader on a journey through the subtle art and profound science of influencing different people's thoughts and opinions. This investigation dives into the fundamental principles that govern our capacity to successfully generate persuasive arguments and persuade others, beginning with the classical rhetoric of ancient philosophers and progressing all the way up to the contemporary nuances of cognitive psychology. Join us as we uncover the methods, decipher the strategies, and discover the foundations that have stood the test of time that enable words to influence people's thoughts and opinions.

As a leading lantern through the shadows of rhetoric, "Understanding the Foundations of Persuasion and Argumentation" serves as a guiding lantern in the labyrinth of discourse, where ideas collide and convictions converge. This book does not only examine the surface of persuasion; rather, it excavates the layers beneath, showing the cognitive landscapes where a person's views take root. The delicate fabric of human persuasion is shown in each chapter, beginning with Aristotle's ethos, pathos, and logos triad and progressing all the way to the nuanced dance of framing and priming when it comes to contemporary communication. In the process of navigating the corridors of influence, the narrative threads combine ancient wisdom with cutting-edge ideas in a seamless manner, thus providing a roadmap for readers to interpret the language of conviction. The power of persuasion will be demystified, and the foundations of powerful arguments will be laid naked, as you embark on an enthralling journey of discovery.

CHAPTER 1

The Psychology of Persuasion

Emotional Intelligence

Emotional intelligence (EI) plays a critical role in effective persuasion by allowing individuals to comprehend, manage, and exploit emotions—both their own and others'. Here are key aspects of how emotional intelligence helps to persuade communication

Empathy: High EI enables individuals to empathize with others, understanding their viewpoints, emotions, and needs. This sympathetic awareness allows for better personalized and convincing messages that appeal to the audience on an emotional level.

Self-awareness: People with excellent emotional intelligence have a heightened awareness of their own feelings. This self-awareness helps people moderate their emotional responses during persuasive conversations, ensuring they express authenticity and sincerity.

Social skills: Persuasion frequently entails excellent communication and relationship-building. Individuals with high EI possess good social abilities, enabling them to manage interpersonal dynamics, build rapport, and establish connections that lead to successful persuasion.

Adaptability: Emotionally savvy persons may adjust their communication style to match the emotional tone of their audience. This adaptability strengthens the persuasiveness of their words, as they may resonate with varied emotional states.

Motivation: A strong internal motivation generally accompanies emotional intelligence. Individuals with high EI are driven by a genuine concern for others' well-being and success, promoting trust and credibility in their persuasive attempts.

Regulation of Emotions: Effective persuasion includes managing emotions, both one's own and those of others. Emotional intelligence helps individuals regulate emotions, avoiding negative emotions from derailing the persuasive process and facilitating a more positive and receptive atmosphere.

Non-verbal Communication: A substantial percentage of communication is non-verbal, including facial expressions, body language, and tone of voice. Emotional intelligence aids in decoding and employing these non-verbal cues effectively during persuasion, boosting the overall impact of the message.

In essence, emotional intelligence promotes persuasion by increasing empathy, self-awareness, adaptability, and effective communication. Individuals with high EI can connect with others on a deeper emotional level, making their persuasive attempts more powerful and influential.

Insights into Human Behavior

Insights into human behavior cover a vast array of observations and understandings obtained from numerous fields. Here are fundamental observations about human behavior:

Cognitive Processes: The study of cognitive psychology provides insights into how humans perceive, process information, and make decisions. Understanding cognitive processes helps untangle the subtleties of learning, memory, problem-solving, and decision-making.

Emotional Dynamics: Emotions play a crucial part in human behavior. Insights from psychology explain how emotions influence our ideas and actions, impacting social interactions, relationships, and overall well-being.

Social Influence: Social psychology investigates the impact of others on individual behavior. Concepts like conformity, obedience, and social standards shed light on how people are influenced by the presence and conduct of those around them.

Cultural Variations: Anthropological studies give insights into how culture impacts human behavior. Examining cultural norms, beliefs, and rituals helps comprehend both universal and culture-specific aspects of behavior.

Motivation and Drives: Psychology and neuroscience examine the variables that drive human behavior, such as wants, desires, and intrinsic motivations. Understanding what motivates individuals is vital in predicting and influencing their actions.

Group Dynamics: Sociology dives into group behavior and dynamics, illustrating how individuals interact within broader social institutions. Concepts like social identity, roles, and institutions provide insights into collective behavior.

Neurobiological Foundations: Neuroscience investigates the biological basis of behavior. Insights into brain architecture, neurotransmitters, and genetic variables contribute to understanding the physiological bases of certain behaviors.

Developmental Perspectives: Examining human behavior across the lifetime provides insights into how humans evolve and grow. Developmental psychology finds patterns of behavior from infancy to old age, demonstrating the impact of different life stages.

Communication Patterns: Insights from communication studies show how verbal and non-verbal communication impacts human interaction. Understanding communication dynamics helps interpret messages and negotiate interpersonal relationships.

Adaptability and Resilience: Behavioral science recognizes the human capability for adaptability and resilience in the face of adversities. Studying how individuals cope with adversity provides insights into the strength and flexibility of human behavior.

These ideas collectively contribute to a holistic view of human behavior, reflecting the interplay of psychological, social, cultural, and biological variables that affect individuals and civilizations.

CHAPTER 2

Crafting Compelling Arguments

Formulating a Solid Thesis

Formulating a sound thesis is a critical step in academic writing, requiring careful attention and precision. Here are crucial factors to bear in mind while creating a powerful thesis statement:

Clarity and Conciseness: Clearly articulate the main point or argument of your article in a brief manner. A great thesis should explain your position without extra intricacy, ensuring readers comprehend your primary claim.

Specificity: Avoid vague or generic comments. A great thesis is specific and focused, providing a clear indication of what the paper will address. Clearly describe the scope and bounds of your argument.

Debatable and Defensible: A robust thesis statement gives an argument that is open to debate and discussion. Avoid expressing facts or universally accepted truths; instead, aim for a viewpoint that invites analysis and counterarguments.

Narrow Scope: Focus on a certain area of your topic rather than attempting to cover too much ground. A focused and well-defined thesis allows for a more in-depth investigation of the subject within the limits of your work.

Evidential Support: Your thesis should be supported by evidence and examples. Consider the research or data that backs your claim, ensuring your thesis is anchored in meaningful material that improves your entire case.

Originality: Strive to offer a fresh perspective or a unique insight into the topic. Avoid clichés and generic remarks, aiming for a thesis that brings something new or challenges existing ideas.

Awareness of Counterarguments: Acknowledge probable counter arguments or different opinions. A strong thesis indicates a comprehension of the intricacy of the problem and frames your argument within the broader conversation.

Logical Flow: Your thesis should give a roadmap for the reader, summarizing the important ideas that will be discussed in the work. Ensure that the structure of your thesis coincides with the logical flow of your arguments.

Relevance: Ensure that your thesis remains relevant to the broader aim of your article. Each component of your argument should tie directly to your thesis statement, keeping a cohesive and logical narrative.

Revision and Refinement: Crafting a great thesis is an iterative process. Be prepared to alter and refine your argument as you go deeper into your research and writing. Your thesis may evolve as your understanding of the topic matures.

By incorporating these parts into your thesis statement, you may construct a firm foundation for your academic writing, giving a roadmap for both yourself and your readers as you investigate and expand your arguments.

Building a Logical Framework

Building a logical framework is necessary for structuring plans, projects, or arguments in a clear and systematic fashion. Here's a guide to help you develop a logical framework:

Define the Purpose and Objectives:
- Clearly articulate the purpose and overarching objectives of your strategy or project.
- State the targeted goals, impact, or changes you hope to achieve.

Identify Inputs, Activities, and Outputs:
- List the resources, inputs, or components necessary for the accomplishment of your plan.
- Outline the exact activities or actions that will be conducted.
- Define the tangible outcomes or deliverables that result from these actions.

Establish Assumptions and Risks:
- Identify any assumptions or conditions that are crucial for the success of your plan.
- Recognize any dangers or barriers that could hamper growth.
- Develop ways to mitigate risks and eventualities.

Create a Logical Framework Matrix: Construct a matrix that visually organizes critical aspects, harmonizing aims, outputs, activities, indicators, means of verification, and assumptions. This matrix gives an organized overview, ensuring that each element contributes logically to the broader plan.

Define Indicators and Means of Verification:

- Develop measurable indicators that objectively assess progress toward objectives.
- Specify the means of verification, indicating how you will collect data or proof to measure each indication.

Establish a Results Chain: Outline the causal relationship between inputs, activities, outputs, outcomes, and total impact.

Clarify how each component helps to obtain the next level of results.

Ensure SMART Criteria: Make targets Specific, Measurable, Achievable, Relevant, and Time-bound, this ensures that your goals are well-defined and feasible, supporting effective planning and evaluation.

Monitor and Evaluate: Develop a monitoring and evaluation plan to methodically track progress.

Establish regular checkpoints to review whether objectives are being fulfilled and adjust the plan as needed.

Incorporate Stakeholder Involvement

- Engage important stakeholders in the logical framework creation process.
- Consider their viewpoints, knowledge, and contributions to strengthen the robustness of your plan.

Iterative Refinement: Recognize that the logical framework is not static. It may need refinement as circumstances change or new information becomes available.

Continuously assess and update the framework to ensure its continued relevance and effectiveness.

Building a logical framework gives a disciplined method to planning and executing initiatives, fostering clarity, responsibility, and effective communication throughout the process.

CHAPTER 3

Effective Communication Strategies

The Art of Verbal Persuasion

The art of verbal persuasion is a sophisticated skill that entails using language effectively to influence and convince people. Here are crucial elements to master in the art of verbal persuasion

Clarity of Message: Clearly articulate your message. A well-defined and unambiguous message is more likely to resonate with your audience.

Understanding Your Audience: Tailor your message to the individual requirements, interests, and values of your audience. Understanding your listeners boosts the relevance and impact of your argument.

Building Credibility: Establish credibility by displaying your expertise, knowledge, or experience on the topic. A credible speaker is more likely to be persuasive.

Affective link: Evoke the emotions of your audience. Emotional connections can improve the impact of your message and make it more memorable.

Effective Use of Language: Choose your words wisely. Use language that is intriguing, vivid, and resonates with your audience. Avoid jargon that may alienate or confuse.

Storytelling: Craft interesting stories that demonstrate your views. Narratives have a profound effect on human psychology and can boost the persuasiveness of your message.

Active Listening: Demonstrate active listening by expressing genuine interest in others' viewpoints. Understanding their opinions allows you to adjust your persuasive technique more successfully.

Establishing Common Ground: Find common ground with your audience. Shared beliefs or interests create a foundation for persuasion and build a sense of solidarity.

Use of Rhetorical Techniques: Employ rhetorical techniques such as analogies, metaphors, and similes. These technologies can make your message more memorable and appealing.

Handling Objections: Anticipate and answer any objections. Acknowledging and addressing opposition arguments indicates diligence and boosts your credibility.

Confidence and Conviction: Speak with confidence and conviction. A convincing speaker emanates assurance, which can positively influence the audience's perception of the message.

Non-Verbal Communication: Pay attention to your body language, tone of voice, and gestures. Non-verbal clues can dramatically affect how your message is received.

Timing and tempo: Consider the timing and tempo of your speech. A well-timed message delivered at a suitable tempo can boost its efficacy.

Call to Action: Clearly describe what you want your audience to do or believe after hearing your message. A compelling call to action provides direction and purpose.

Adaptability: Be adaptable in your approach. Read the room and change your persuasive methods based on the dynamics of the scenario.

Mastering the art of verbal persuasion needs a mix of excellent communication skills, emotional intelligence, and a grasp of human psychology. By developing these elements, you can become a more compelling and influential speaker.

Non-Verbal Communication Tactics

Non-verbal communication strategies play a key role in transmitting messages, altering perceptions, and developing effective interpersonal connections. Here are key methods to promote non-verbal communication:

Physique Communication: Observe the way one carries themselves, their gestures, and facial expressions. Open and confident body language improves trustworthiness and engagement.

Eye Contact: Maintain acceptable eye contact. It expresses honesty, attentiveness, and confidence. However, be aware not to stare, as it may be viewed as frightening.

Facial Expression: Express emotions genuinely through facial expressions. A sincere smile, arched eyebrows, or a thoughtful look can give depth to your conversation.

Motions: Use deliberate motions to accentuate points or add emphasis. Be conscious of cultural variations to ensure gestures are universally understood.

Proximity and Personal Space: Be aware of personal space. Respect people's comfort zones to prevent making them feel crowded or uncomfortable.

Touch: Use touch wisely and observe cultural standards. A handshake, pat on the back, or other suitable gestures can show warmth and connection.

Mirroring: Mirroring entails gently copying someone's body language. It generates a sense of rapport and connection by signaling resemblance and understanding.

Stance: Maintain an erect and open stance. Slouching or crossing arms can show disinterest or defensiveness.

Appearance: Dress appropriately for the situation and audience. Your wardrobe contributes to the overall impression you convey.

Tone of Voice: Pay attention to your tone, pitch, and tempo. A well-modulated voice that corresponds with the message can boost communication efficacy.

Silence: Embrace moments of silence deliberately. Silence may accentuate points, allow for thinking, and provide a more impactful communication experience.

Adaptability: Adjust your non-verbal cues depending on the cultural setting and the individuals you are interacting with. Diverse cultures might perceive gestures and expressions in varying ways.

Consistency with Verbal Message: Ensure that your non-verbal clues correspond with your spoken message. Inconsistencies might lead to confusion or affect the trustworthiness of your communication.

Nodding: Use slight nods to convey agreement, comprehension, or encouragement. It implies active listening and participation.

Regulate Emotions: Practice emotional regulation using non-verbal clues. Maintain composure in stressful situations to communicate professionalism and resilience.

Visual Aids: When presenting, use visual aids successfully. Pointing to charts or slides can complement spoken communication and boost understanding.

By learning these non-verbal communication strategies, individuals can dramatically boost their capacity to express messages, develop relationships, and influence others positively. These methods are valuable in numerous contexts, from professional settings to personal connections.

CHAPTER 4

Handling Counterarguments

Anticipating and Addressing Opposition
Anticipating and addressing opposition is a fundamental part of effective communication and persuasion. Here's guidance on how to negotiate and respond to probable concerns or resistance:

Research and Preparation: Thoroughly research your audience, stakeholders, or opponents to anticipate probable objections. Understand their viewpoints and concerns beforehand.

Active Listening: During talks, actively listen to others. Pay attention to verbal and non-verbal signs, allowing you to discover potential places of disagreement or conflict.

Empathy: Put yourself in the shoes of individuals who may oppose your opinions. Understanding their opinions helps you adapt your comments more effectively.

Acknowledge Concerns: Start by acknowledging and respecting opposing perspectives. Demonstrating that you understand and appreciate other opinions creates the framework for meaningful communication.

Clarify Misunderstandings: Clarify any misconceptions or misunderstandings that may contribute to opposition. Clear communication helps bridge gaps and creates a more accurate understanding of your perspective.

Address Core Issues: Identify the core issues underlying opposition. Addressing fundamental problems is more successful than merely reacting to surface-level objections.

Provide Evidence and Examples: Support your stance with relevant evidence, data, or examples. Concrete proof supports your case and helps rebut opposing ideas.

Highlight Shared Goals: Emphasize mutual goals and interests. Finding areas of agreement can develop bridges and lower the intensity of antagonism.

Use Analogies and Comparisons: Frame your case using analogies or comparisons that resonate with your audience. Analogies can simplify difficult ideas and make them more approachable.

Engage in productive Dialogue: Encourage open and productive dialogue. Create an environment where individuals feel comfortable sharing issues, encouraging a more collaborative atmosphere.

Offer Compromises: Be open to finding a middle ground or compromise where possible. Flexibility in your position can assist lessen objections and lead to more cooperative solutions.

Anticipate Frequently Asked Questions (FAQs): Develop responses to anticipated frequently asked questions. This proactive strategy helps you to address concerns before they are mentioned.

Remain Calm and Respectful: Maintain composure and remain respectful, especially in the face of strong resistance. Emotional intelligence is vital in defusing tension and developing effective talks.

Use Positive Language: Frame your responses positively. Positive language is more likely to be perceived warmly and can help to a more fruitful discourse.

Seek comments: Encourage comments and input from people who reject your ideas.

Actively seeking input demonstrates a willingness to engage in a collaborative process.

Iterative Communication: Be prepared to revisit and adjust your communication strategy based on the shifting nature of the topic. Iterative communication enables ongoing improvement.

Anticipating and confronting opposition involves a combination of preparation, empathy, and effective communication tactics. By proactively addressing objections, you strengthen your ability to develop consensus, overcome resistance, and achieve effective outcomes.

Strengthening Your Position

Strengthening your position in every debate, negotiation, or argument involves strategic communication, persuasion, and a thorough presentation of your ideas. Here are crucial tactics to bolster your stance:

Research and Knowledge: Thoroughly research the topic area. A well-informed perspective backed by credible evidence lends weight to your argument.

Clarity of Message: Clearly describe your primary themes. A succinct and well-defined statement promotes understanding and supports the strength of your argument.

Identify Core Strengths: Identify and stress the core strengths of your stance. Clearly describe the specific advantages or benefits that support your perspective.

Anticipate Opposition: Anticipate potential concerns and address them proactively. This exhibits insight and improves your position by preemptively resolving worries.

Use Persuasive Language: Choose language that is persuasive and impactful. Frame your ideas in a way that resonates with your audience and evokes support.

Provide Evidence and Examples: Support your position using relevant evidence, statistics, or real-world examples. Concrete proof lends credibility and persuasiveness to your stance.

Build a captivating Narrative: Craft a captivating narrative around your stance. Storytelling can make your message more memorable and emotionally resonant.

Highlight experience: Showcase your experience on the subject. Establishing yourself as a knowledgeable authority boosts the credibility of your viewpoint.

Stress Shared ideals: Emphasize shared ideals or common ground with your audience. Aligning your perspective with commonly held views generates a sense of oneness.

Use Visuals: Incorporate visuals such as charts, graphs, or diagrams to illustrate crucial concepts. Visual aids can boost understanding and emphasize the strength of your position.

Remain Open to Feedback: Demonstrate a desire to listen and engage in productive discourse. Being receptive to feedback can boost your position by exhibiting adaptability and a collaborative approach.

Highlight Consequences: Articulate the potential consequences or advantages associated with your perspective. Clarifying the impact underscores the relevance of your stance.

Confidence and Assertiveness: Project confidence and assertiveness in your communication. A strong and assured speech can build confidence in others regarding the legitimacy of your stance.

Strategic Alliances: Identify and develop alliances with others who support or share similar positions. A unified voice can boost the overall impact of your stance.

Address Counterarguments: Anticipate and address counterarguments directly. Acknowledging different opinions and delivering reasoned responses indicates the robustness of your position.

Consistency: Ensure consistency in your messaging. A concise and consistent presentation reinforces the reliability of your position.

review and modify: Regularly review the efficacy of your communication strategy and be willing to modify based on feedback or changing circumstances.

By using these tactics, you can solidify your position, boost persuasiveness, and successfully express the value or legitimacy of your opinion to others.

CHAPTER 5

Ethical Considerations in Persuasion

Maintaining Integrity in Argumentation

Maintaining integrity in arguments is vital for building trust, credibility, and healthy conversation. Here are crucial rules to keep ethical standards while presenting and defending your ideas:

Honesty and Transparency: Always be truthful in delivering information. Transparency about your sources, facts, and potential biases fosters confidence and trust with your audience.

Avoid Misrepresentation: Refrain from manipulating or misrepresenting facts to support your point. Present information accurately, especially if it opposes your perspective.

Acknowledge Limitations: Recognize the limitations of your argument or evidence. Acknowledging uncertainty or gaps in your understanding demonstrates intellectual honesty.

Fairness and Objectivity: Approach the debate with fairness and objectivity. Consider many perspectives, and give a balanced view rather than manipulating information to favor your stance.

Respect for Others' Ideas: Treat opposing viewpoints with respect. Avoid ad hominem attacks and focus on discussing concepts rather than attacking individuals personally.

Avoid Logical Fallacies: Familiarize yourself with basic logical fallacies and endeavor to avoid them. Using erroneous reasoning damages the integrity of your argument.

Cite Sources Properly: Provide accurate and proper citations for every content you use. Plagiarism weakens your credibility and defies ethical standards.

Clarity and Precision: Clearly communicate your views and ensure precision in wording. Vague or imprecise comments might lead to misunderstandings and weaken the integrity of your argument.

Ethical Use of Persuasion: Use ethical persuasion strategies. Manipulating emotions or adopting misleading strategies erodes confidence and destroys the integrity of your conversation.

Consistency in Ideals: Ensure consistency in your ethical ideals. Apply the same standards of honesty to all areas of your argument, including evidence, logic, and presentation.

Disclose Conflicts of Interest: Disclose any potential conflicts of interest that could impact your position. Transparency regarding personal or financial links improves trust.

Admit Mistakes: If you identify errors in your argument, admit them freely. Correcting mistakes indicates humility and a commitment to truth over ego.

Promote productive Dialogue: Encourage open and productive dialogue. Foster an environment where varied viewpoints can be shared without fear of punishment.

Stay Informed: Stay informed and updated on the topic matter. A well-informed argument is more likely to survive criticism and keep its integrity.

Reflect Ethical Values: Ensure that your argument resonates with ethical values. Consider the broader ethical ramifications of your position on individuals and society.

Consider Long-Term Impact: Think about the long-term impact of your argument. Consider how it may contribute positively or negatively to the discourse and the community at large.
By continuously respecting these rules, you not only retain the integrity of your argument but also contribute to a culture of ethical communication and reasoned debate.

Responsible Persuasion Practices

Responsible persuasion tactics incorporate ethical and attentive communication approaches aimed at influencing people while retaining integrity and respect. Here are fundamental ideas for guiding responsible persuasion:

Transparency: Be transparent about your aims and motives. Clearly communicate the aim of your persuasion to develop trust with your audience.

Appreciate Autonomy: Acknowledge and appreciate the autonomy of your audience. Allow individuals the freedom to make their own decisions without undue coercion.

Informed Consent: Ensure that your audience is well-informed about the information you present. Avoid influencing or fooling individuals to gain consent.

Empathy: Understand and empathize with the thoughts and feelings of your audience. This helps adapt your message to be more attentive and relevant.

Cultural Sensitivity: Be mindful of cultural nuances and variances. Tailor your persuasive strategy to accord with the cultural norms and sensitivities of your audience.

Avoid Exploitation: Refrain from exploiting vulnerabilities or manipulating emotions to attain your goals. Responsible persuasion tries to empower rather than take advantage of others.

Focus on Shared Ideals: Emphasize shared ideals and common ground. Responsible persuasion strives to find commonality rather than exploit differences for selfish advantage.

Truthfulness: Uphold truthfulness in your conversation. Avoid spreading disinformation or distorting facts to buttress your stance.

Consider Long-Term Repercussions: Think about the long-term repercussions of your persuasive efforts. Responsible persuasion addresses the broader influence on relationships, trust, and societal well-being.

Open Discourse: Encourage open discourse and the exchange of varied ideas. Responsible persuasion includes creating an environment where differing viewpoints can be voiced and valued.

Accountability: Take responsibility for the outcomes of your persuasive efforts. If unanticipated negative outcomes develop, be willing to address and rectify them.

Resist Manipulative Techniques: Avoid utilizing manipulative techniques or psychological strategies that exploit cognitive biases. Responsible persuasion relies on ethical and honest communication.

Consider the Well-being of Others: Prioritize the well-being of your audience. Responsible persuasive tactics examine the impact on persons' mental, emotional, and physical well-being.

Adaptability: Be adaptable in your approach. Responsible persuasion realizes that varied contexts and audiences may demand variations in tactics.

Promote Critical Thinking: Encourage critical thinking rather than seeking uncritical acquiescence. Responsible persuasion helps individuals to think critically and make informed decisions.

Responsible Use of Technology: When utilizing technology for persuasion, ensure responsible and ethical behaviors. Avoid the manipulation of algorithms or the distribution of incorrect information.

Continuous Reflection: Reflect on your persuasive methods periodically. Consider how your procedures accord with ethical norms and whether adjustments are needed.

Responsible persuasion is built in ethical communication, empathy, and genuine care for the well-being of others. By embracing these ideas, you can influence positively while retaining a dedication to honesty and respect.

CHAPTER 6

Persuasion in Various Contexts

Professional Settings

In professional settings, effective persuasion is a valuable talent that entails persuading others in a manner consistent with ethical and professional standards. Here are crucial considerations for persuasion in professional environments:

Understanding Your Audience: Tailor your persuasive strategy to the specific needs, interests, and concerns of your professional audience. Consider their jobs, priorities, and viewpoints to develop a convincing message.

Building Credibility: Establish and retain credibility in professional contexts. Your professional reputation, skills, and track record considerably influence how your persuasive attempts are regarded.

Emphasizing Professionalism: Maintain a high level of professionalism in both your communication style and approach. Professionalism boosts your persuasiveness and reinforces your trustworthiness.

Clear and Concise Communication: Professional situations necessitate clear and concise communication. Present your arguments in a systematic and easily understood manner, respecting others' time and attention.

Aligning With Organizational Aims: Ensure that your persuasive efforts align with the overarching aims and values of the organization. This congruence boosts the relevancy and acceptance of your message.

Collaborative Approach: Adopt a collaborative approach to persuasion. Emphasize how your plan or concept helps the team or business as a whole, promoting a sense of shared achievement.

Incorporating Data and Evidence: Use appropriate data, evidence, and examples to support your ideas. In professional settings, decision-makers generally prefer evidence-based recommendations.

Respecting Hierarchy: Be conscious of corporate hierarchy and the decision-making framework. Tailor your persuasive technique based on the professional levels of your audience.

Active Listening: Demonstrate active listening abilities to comprehend the concerns and opinions of your colleagues or superiors. Addressing their demands and adding their feedback boosts your persuasiveness.

Handling Objections Properly: Anticipate objections and respond to them properly. Address concerns with evidence, intelligent explanations, and a focus on finding solutions.

Strategic Timing: Consider the timing of your persuasive attempts. Present your proposals or thoughts during times when your audience is attentive and able to give thorough consideration.

Professional Networking: Leverage professional networks to support your persuasive efforts. Building ties within the organization might provide allies who may advocate for your views.

Adaptability and Flexibility: Be adaptive in your persuasive technique. Professional environments often involve dynamic conditions, and flexibility in your technique is crucial to negotiating change.

Ethical Considerations: Uphold ethical norms in your persuasion attempts. Avoid deceptive tactics or misleading information, as ethical conduct is vital in professional contexts.

Feedback and Iteration: Seek feedback on your persuasive efforts and be open to iterate based on input. Continuous development is a hallmark of effective persuasion in professional contexts.

Measuring Impact: Assess the impact of your persuasive efforts on organizational goals. Measure success in terms of good results and contributions to the organization's success.

In professional settings, effective persuasion is not just about accomplishing individual goals but also about contributing to the overall performance and objectives of the business. Balancing professionalism, trustworthiness, and strategic communication is crucial to becoming a persuasive and powerful professional.

Personal Relationships

Persuasion in personal relationships entails persuading others in a respectful and considerate manner. Whether it is friendships, family dynamics, or romantic connections, effective persuasion can deepen relationships. Here are crucial principles for persuasion in personal contexts:

Understanding Personal Dynamics: Recognize the unique dynamics and communication styles within your personal connections. Tailor your persuasive strategy based on the specific tastes and sensitivities of the people concerned.

Empathy and Emotional Intelligence: Demonstrate empathy and emotional intelligence. Understand the feelings and viewpoints of people, and utilize this insight to shape your persuasive attempts with care.

Transparent and Truthful Dialogue: Encourage transparent and truthful dialogue. Transparency and authenticity generate trust, which is vital in personal interactions.

Active Listening: Practice active listening to comprehend the worries, desires, and wants of the other person. Being attentive and responsive boosts the effectiveness of your persuasive attempts.

Respecting Boundaries: Be conscious of personal boundaries. Persuasion should respect the autonomy and individual decisions of others within the boundaries of the interaction.

Timing and Patience: Choose the correct timing for your persuasive arguments. Exercise patience and analyze the emotional state of the other person to create an environment receptive to persuading.

Mutual Benefit: Emphasize mutual benefit. Clearly express how your plan or concept benefits both parties, establishing a sense of shared interest and teamwork.

Building Trust: Trust is important in human interactions. Your persuasive attempts should coincide with your past behaviors, reinforcing the trust that has been developed over time.

Seeking Win-Win Solutions: Aim for win-win solutions in your persuasive interactions. Prioritize outcomes that are favorable for both parties, establishing a harmonious partnership.

Understanding Motivations: Understand the motivations and values of the other person. Aligning your persuasive attempts with their underlying ideas boosts the likelihood of a positive reaction.

Using Positive Reinforcement: Employ positive reinforcement to encourage desirable actions. Recognizing and respecting the strengths and efforts of the other person develops a helpful environment.

Acknowledging Emotions: Acknowledge and validate the emotions of the other person. Recognition of their feelings indicates empathy and adds to a more receptive mindset.

Conflict Resolution Abilities: Develop effective conflict resolution abilities. In personal relationships, disagreements are unavoidable, and the capacity to negotiate conflicts constructively enriches the partnership.

Admitting Mistakes: Be willing to admit mistakes and take responsibility for any misconceptions. Humility and accountability contribute to a good and resilient relationship.

Balancing Independence and Interdependence: Recognize the importance of both individual autonomy and common goals.

Striking a balance between independence and interdependence contributes to the strength of the connection.

Continued Communication: Establish a habit of continual communication. Regular check-ins, updates, and talks ensure that both sides are on the same page and can contribute to a pleasant and expanding relationship.

Cultural Sensitivity: Consider cultural differences within the connection. Awareness of cultural differences enhances understanding and helps avoid misconceptions in your persuasive encounters.

In personal relationships, persuasive efforts should be built with respect, empathy, and a genuine desire for mutual well-being. Building and maintaining positive friendships involve effective communication and a commitment to understanding and supporting one another.

CHAPTER 7

Overcoming Common Challenges

Dealing with Resistance

Addressing resistance in persuasion is a sophisticated process that requires understanding the concerns of the other person and navigating through obstacles. Here are useful ways for coping with resistance in compelling situations:

Active Listening: Begin by actively listening to the concerns and objections of the resistant party. Paying attention and displaying understanding sets the stage for good communication.

Empathize And Validate: Show empathy and validate the emotions or concerns of the resistive individual. Acknowledging their feelings fosters a more compassionate and collaborative atmosphere.

Clarify Objectives: Clearly articulate the objectives and benefits of the proposed proposal or change. Ensuring that the reluctant party understands the aim helps mitigate misunderstandings.

Provide Additional Information: Offer additional information or data that addresses specific concerns. Providing a more detailed understanding of the situation helps reduce doubts and develop trust.

Acknowledge and Address Concerns: Acknowledge particular concerns stated by the resisting party and address them directly. This indicates your commitment to resolving conflicts and finding common ground.

Build Rapport: Strengthen your relationship with the resistive individual. Building rapport develops trust, making it more likely that they will be open to considering your position.

Present Alternatives: Offer alternative options or concessions. Providing options encourages the reluctant party to feel more involved in the decision-making process.

Focus on Common Aims: Emphasize similar aims and interests. Highlighting common ground helps to reframe the problem as a collaborative effort rather than a subject of disagreement.

Involve Others: If appropriate, involve other stakeholders or individuals who may share similar perspectives. A communal approach might sometimes lessen resistance by exhibiting broader support.

Highlight Good Outcomes: Clearly express the good outcomes or benefits that may result from accepting the suggested proposal. Illustrate how it coincides with the interests of the resisting party.

Address Fears and Uncertainties: If resistance originates from fears or uncertainties, address these directly. Providing comfort and resolving underlying worries can be crucial to overcoming reluctance.

Provide a Test or Trial Term: Propose a trial term or pilot project to allow the resistive party to experience the changes on a smaller scale. This can help reduce fears and create confidence.

Educate and Inform: Offer instructional resources or information sessions to promote comprehension. Sometimes, resistance stems from a lack of understanding, and sharing information can be instructive.

Seek Comments: Encourage the resistive party to provide comments and suggestions. Involving them in the decision-making process makes them feel more valued and can lead to better outcomes.

Be Patient and Persistent: Dealing with resistance takes time. Be patient and persistent in your efforts, realizing that it may require numerous discussions to obtain a conclusion.

Applaud Minor Wins: Acknowledge and applaud any progress or agreement, no matter how minor. Recognizing achievements builds good momentum and fosters cooperation.

Examine and Alter: Periodically examine the situation and be open to altering your approach. Flexibility and a readiness to adapt demonstrate your dedication to finding mutually accepted solutions.

Dealing with opposition in persuasion involves a blend of empathy, good communication, and a real commitment to addressing issues. By employing these tactics, you may manage opposition more successfully and achieve consensus in persuasive situations.

Adapting to Different Audiences

Adapting to varied audiences is a critical ability that increases effective communication and persuasion. Here are key techniques to customize your message for varied audiences:

Audience Study: Conduct a detailed audience study to determine the demographics, interests, values, and expectations of your audience. Tailor your messaging based on these insights.

Customize Language and Tone: Adjust your language and tone to reflect the preferences and communication style of the target audience. Use vocabulary and expressions that resonate with them.

Cultural Sensitivity: Be conscious of cultural differences. Consider cultural variations in communication, body language, and customs to avoid misunderstandings and connect more effectively.

Addressing Different Learning Styles: Recognize and accommodate varied learning styles. Some folks may prefer visual aids, while others may learn better through spoken explanations. Use a range of approaches to appeal to varied preferences.

Adapt to Professional Levels: Tailor your message based on the professional levels of your audience. Adjust the level of technical detail, formality, or complexity to correspond with their knowledge and background.

Understand Motivations: Identify the motivations and goals of your audience. Frame your message to align with their interests and objectives, explaining how your ideas or proposals benefit them directly.

Consider Age Groups: Take into account the age groups of your audience. Different generations may have diverse communication preferences and values. Tailor your approach to resonate with the experiences and opinions of each age group.

Adapt to Context: Consider the context in which the conversation is taking place. Whether it's a formal presentation, casual discussion, or written communication, alter your approach properly.

Emphasize Relevance: Highlight the relevance of your message to the targeted audience. Demonstrating how your ideas directly touch their interests or worries boosts engagement.

Addressing Personal Values: Be aware of the values relevant to your audience. Frame your message in a way that aligns with those ideals, building a relationship based on shared ideas.

Tailor Examples and Analogies: Use examples and analogies that resonate with the experiences and interests of your audience. This makes your message more relatable and easy to understand.

Adjust Pace and Timing: Be attentive to the pace of your speech. Some audiences may prefer a faster pace, while others may appreciate a more deliberate and careful approach.

Interactive Engagement: Encourage interaction and engagement. Some audiences may respond well to open talks, while others may prefer more structured approaches. Adapt your strategy to foster participation.

Seek Input: Actively seek input from your audience. Understanding their reactions and impressions allows you to make real-time modifications and strengthen future discussions.

Flexibility in Q&A Sessions: Be flexible during question-and-answer sessions. Adapt your responses based on the questions and concerns made by the audience to ensure clarity and address specific points of interest.

Continuous Learning: Continuously learn from your experiences with different audiences. Reflect on what went well and what may be improved, enhancing your approach for future interactions.

By changing your communication style to the specific qualities and preferences of diverse audiences, you boost your capacity to connect, engage, and convince effectively in varied settings.

CHAPTER 8

Case Studies in Persuasion Success

Real-Life Examples and Analyses

Certainly! Here are two real-life examples of adapting to different audiences, along with assessments of the tactics employed:

Example 1: Professional Presentation

Context: An executive is presenting a presentation to a diverse team of experts within a major corporation. The audience includes personnel from numerous departments, each with different levels of knowledge.

Customized Language: The CEO utilizes a balance of technical vocabulary for professionals in the industry while providing plain explanations for those less knowledgeable. This ensures that all team members can follow the presentation.

Interactive Components: To engage the diverse audience, the presentation includes interactive components such as polls and Q&A

sessions. This allows people to actively engage, making the topic more accessible and relatable.

Visual Aids: Recognizing varied learning styles, the executive inserts visual aids like charts and graphs for people who comprehend material better through visuals, boosting the overall comprehension of the topic.

Analysis: This technique adapts to the diverse professional levels and learning preferences of the audience. The use of tailored language, interactive components, and visual aids ensures that the presentation is inclusive and effectively transmits the desired message to all team members.

Example 2: Community Outreach Campaign

Context: A non-profit group is conducting a community outreach program targeted at addressing health concerns. The target audience comprises persons from varied age ranges, cultural backgrounds, and socioeconomic positions.

Cultural Sensitivity: The marketing materials are designed to be culturally sensitive, reflecting the varied backgrounds of the population. Information is presented in several languages, and cultural nuances are honored.

Tailored Messaging: Messages are intended to resonate with different age groups. For instance, children are targeted with messages highlighting the value of communal well-being, while older persons receive information on the health benefits related to their age.

Accessible Formats: Recognizing socioeconomic variations, the campaign provides accessibility by disseminating information through numerous channels, including community events, printed materials, and digital platforms, reaching a broad population.

Analysis: This advertising exhibits an understanding of the diverse demographics within the community. By personalizing communications, addressing cultural sensitivities, and distributing information through multiple media, the organization maximizes the reach and effectiveness of its health efforts.

In both situations, the key is to identify the diversity within the audience and adopt adaptive tactics to ensure effective communication adapted to the individual requirements and preferences of each group.

CHAPTER 9

Mastering the Art in the Digital Age

Persuasion in Online Communication
Persuasion in online communication involves special tactics due to the nature of virtual interactions. Here are crucial aspects for effectively persuading in an online context:
Clarity and Conciseness: Online viewers have restricted attention spans. Craft simple and succinct communications to swiftly express your important points without overwhelming the audience with extraneous data.
Engaging Visuals: Incorporate engaging visuals such as photos, infographics, or videos. Visual information tends to catch attention and boosts the overall persuasiveness of your argument.
Use of Headlines and Bullet Points: Structure your information with attractive headlines and bullet points. Online readers regularly scan material, and these aspects assist in

highlighting crucial information and make your message more digestible.

Personalization: Personalize your speech by addressing the audience personally. Use their name or refer to specific interests or preferences, if applicable, to create a more individualized relationship.

Interactive Features: Integrate interactive features, such as polls, surveys, or clickable calls to action. Interaction boosts engagement and encourages active participation from your online audience.

Social Proof: Leverage social proof through testimonials, reviews, or recommendations. Online users often rely on the experiences of others to make decisions, making social proof a potent persuasive technique.

Uniformity Across Channels: Maintain uniformity in your messaging across numerous web channels. Whether through emails, social media, or web content, a consistent message generates trust and reinforces your persuasiveness.

Timing and Frequency: Be attentive to the timing and frequency of your messaging. Consider the best periods for online engagement, and avoid overwhelming your audience with too-frequent communications.

Utilize Social Media Platforms: Utilize the advantages of social media platforms to boost persuasion. Utilize storytelling, live videos, and audience participation to establish a dynamic and persuasive online presence.

Data-driven Persuasion: Use data and analytics to optimize your strategy. Monitor online engagement data to determine what works best for your audience and change your persuasive methods accordingly.

Mobile-Friendly Material: Ensure that your material is mobile-friendly. Many customers access online information through mobile devices, and a flexible design delivers a fluid and persuasive experience across various platforms.

Authenticity and Openness: Maintain authenticity and openness in your online communications. Online viewers prefer authentic, honest communication, and it contributes to creating trust.

Storytelling Tactics: Employ storytelling tactics to deliver your message. Narratives develop a connection with your audience and make your compelling message more memorable.

Emphasize Benefits: Clearly define the benefits of your plan or idea. Online users are generally motivated by what they stand to gain, therefore stressing the positive consequences boosts persuasiveness.

Encouragement for Action: Incorporate a concise and compelling invitation to take action. Whether it's pushing a purchase, signing up for a newsletter, or sharing content, a well-crafted call to action drives internet visitors toward desired activities.

Adapt to Digital Culture: Stay alert to digital culture and online trends. Adapting your messaging to correspond with current online norms and behaviors boosts relevance and persuasiveness.

Responsive Communication: Be responsive to comments, messages, and requests. Timely responses indicate a dedication to interaction and add to a great online presence.

By integrating these tactics, you may effectively negotiate the complexities of online communication and boost your capacity to convince and influence your virtual audience.

Navigating Social Media Challenges
Navigating social media challenges in the context of persuasion requires tackling various hurdles that may occur in persuading and engaging audiences online. Here are key ways to solve these challenges:

Addressing unfavorable Feedback: Respond to unfavorable comments with empathy and a commitment to resolution. Use the chance to display transparency and a willingness to address concerns, turning prospective opponents into advocates through constructive participation.

Building Trust in an Online Environment: Consistently produce honest material that resonates with your business values. Utilize testimonials, case studies, and user-generated content to build social proof and establish trust with your online audience.

Balancing Persuasion and Authenticity: Maintain authenticity while convincing your audience. Craft statements that feel genuine, avoiding overtly sales-oriented language. Engage in two-way interactions to develop a more authentic connection with your audience.

Adapting to Algorithm Changes: Stay informed about social media network algorithm changes. Regularly examine performance indicators, change your content strategy based on the shifting algorithms, and leverage sponsored promotions to keep visibility.

Managing Online Reputation: Implement a thorough online reputation management plan. Monitor mentions of your company, respond swiftly to reviews, and actively engage in good online interactions to develop a favorable reputation.

Encouraging Meaningful Engagement: Foster meaningful interactions by offering thought-provoking questions, running polls, and actively reacting to comments. Create material that inspires discussion and encourages your audience to contribute their thoughts.

Ensuring Privacy and Data Protection: Clearly convey your commitment to privacy. Ensure compliance with data protection legislation, establish transparent privacy policies, and aggressively address any privacy issues voiced by your audience.

Navigating Influencer Partnerships: Choose influencers whose ideals coincide with your brand. Prioritize influencers with authentic involvement rather than concentrating exclusively on follower count. Clearly express expectations and establish a collaborative partnership.

Modifying to Virality and Trends: Monitor online trends and be nimble in modifying your material to coincide with popular subjects. Leverage viral material wisely and genuinely to boost your brand's visibility and relevance.

Combating Online Disinformation: Counter disinformation by sharing correct and verified information. Establish your brand as a trusted source of knowledge, and aggressively engage with your audience to correct any misconceptions.

Ensuring Content Compliance: Stay current on platform content restrictions and adhere to them. Regularly examine your material to guarantee compliance, decreasing the chance of content removal or account suspension.

Demonstrating Thought Leadership: Establish yourself or your brand as a thought leader in your field. Share important ideas, participate in topical topics, and exhibit expertise with material that educates and informs your audience.

Strategic Use of Calls-to-Action (CTAs): Utilize clever CTAs to steer your audience towards desired actions. Clearly describe the benefits of taking the suggested action and ensure that CTAs are properly integrated into your persuasive content.

Navigating Cross-Platform Integration in Persuasion: Develop a unified cross-platform persuasion strategy. Tailor your persuasive messaging for each platform while maintaining a consistent brand narrative. Utilize cross-platform campaigns to emphasize essential messaging.

Ethical Persuasion Practices: Uphold ethical principles in your persuasive attempts. Clearly express the value proposition of your items or ideas, avoiding dishonest approaches. Transparency and honesty assist in creating trust.

By implementing these methods into your social media persuasion efforts, you can effectively handle difficulties, build trust with your audience, and create a persuasive online presence.

CONCLUSION

In the closing pages of "Mastering the Art of Persuasion and Argument," we find ourselves at the culmination of a transforming journey. Throughout this investigation of the intricacies of persuasion and argumentation, we've delved into the fundamental ideas and sophisticated tactics that support effective communication. As we close, it's crucial to reflect on the key insights that equip readers to become skilled navigators of discourse.

Mastering persuasion entails not only the expert use of language but also a profound understanding of human behavior, empathy, and ethical issues. We've traveled the landscape of emotional intelligence, understanding its important role in generating captivating narratives and influencing minds. Whether in professional contexts, personal connections, or the enormous terrain of internet communication, the capacity to adapt and connect with varied audiences stands as a cornerstone of persuasive competence.

In the art of argumentation, we've covered the development of solid theses, logical frameworks, and the delicate balance between reason and emotion. The voyage has led us through the complexities of verbal and non-verbal communication, anticipating opposition, and bolstering one's position with integrity. We've found the essence of ethical persuasive tactics and the need to preserve authenticity, especially in the face of obstacles.

The tapestry of this investigation extends beyond mere rhetoric—it involves the cultivation of critical thinking, the elegant dance of negotiation, and the deliberate deployment of influence in both professional and personal realms. The book has aimed to equip readers not only with the ability to explain their viewpoints successfully but also with the wisdom to negotiate the complexity of human connection with delicacy.

As we complete the chapter on "Mastering the Art of Persuasion and Argument," let these concepts resonate in your activities. The road to mastering persuasion and argumentation is constant, distinguished by a commitment to lifelong learning, adaptation, and an uncompromising fidelity to ethical communication. May the ideas inside these pages serve as a guiding compass for readers, helping them to sail the oceans of conversation with confidence, clarity, and mastery befitting true persuaders and intelligent arguers.

www.ingramcontent.com/pod-product-compliance
Lightning Source LLC
Chambersburg PA
CBHW031327250726
48656CB00005B/2008